Dedicated To:
Trey

Written By: Abigail Gartland

Hello, my name is St. Maximilian Kolbe!

That is kind of a hard name to say, so let's practice together!

Max-uh-mil-e-un

Nice job!

I was born in Poland in 1894.

When I was only 12 years old, I had a vision from our mother, Mary!

She showed me two different crowns that showed how my life would be.

Mary our mother asked which one I wanted, either purity or martyrdom and I decided on both!

One year later, my brother and I joined the Franciscans

After a few years, I finally became a priest!

A few years later, I returned to Poland.

Poland had been invaded, and we were taken to a scary place away from our home.

I was very scared, but I knew that Jesus and Mary were with me.

One day, someone was about to be very hurt, but I volunteered to take his place.

The man was very grateful. I was not scared at all because Jesus and Mary were with me.

I went to Heaven and met Mary and Jesus on August 14, 1941.

Do you want to me more like me?

Anytime that you become scared, you can ask Jesus and Mary for some help!

You can always ask me for my help as well! I am the patron saint of families and many other things!

When you are a little bit older, you can learn much more about me. I pray for you every day of your life.

St. Maximilian Kolbe pray for us!

Copyright:

Clipart: © PentoolPixie © LimeandKiwiDesigns
Licensed purchased: 1/10/2024

About the Author

Abigail Gartland

I love the saints and I love my faith. The idea for sharing the stories of the saints with little ones came when my dear friends were expecting their first baby. I wanted to create something as unique and special as our friendship. Each book is dedicated to very special people and groups who have enriched my faith in different ways. I am blessed to write these stories and appreciate the unending support of my family and friends. When I am not writing, I am a middle school teacher. I hope you enjoy these stories. I pray for each and every person who opens one of my books to learn more about the saints.

Abbie

www.ingramcontent.com/pod-product-compliance
Lightning Source LLC
LaVergne TN
LVHW020420070526
838199LV00055B/3678